Dedication/Acknowledgements

First, I would like to thank the Creator without HIM nothing is possible. Next, I would like to thank my Barber family, friends, peers and colleagues for their continued support and encouragement. To my immediate Family Nicole, Amber, John III and my first grandson Marcel for being the inspiration for this book. And lastly, I would like to thank all of the children I have given 1st haircuts to, someof which are still my loyal clients to this day. This book is dedicated to my Parents, Grandparents, Family, loyal clients and ALL future children, Parents and TRUE HAIR PROFESSIONALS.

My Child's First Haircut

A Preparation Tool for Children, Parents, and Barbers

ISBN:ISBN 978-0-692936467

My Child's First Haircut

A Preparation Tool for Children, Parents, and Barbers

by John E. Bey, Jr

Contents:

Notice to Parents:

Greetings! I know getting a haircut for the"first" time might not seem like a big deal. But it is an important milestone event for a Child, Parent or Barber. For you the Parent, it serves as a notice that your child is growing up. For your child, it can be scary yet exciting with the right 'preparation." Like any "firsts" it is important to tell your child what to expect so you can assess and approach this issue with a better attitude ahead of time. You will want to communicate and clarify in detail the various things that occur in and around a salon or barbershop. It also will help to instill in the child the importance of overcoming their fears, personal grooming and developing healthy self-esteem. Lastly, it assures the child that the place and person you have chosen can be a safe, clean and fun place to get a haircut from.

1, 2, 3,'s (On Finding a Barber Professional):

1. Asssess (attitude on 1st time haircuts)

2. Behavior (overall)

3. Conversation (general)

4. Dialogue (with you and Child)

5. Experience

6. Flexible (friendly yet firm)

7. Goal-oriented

8. Hygienic

9. Informative (Inspiring and instrumental)

10. Joint-venture (this is a journey ALL must be joyful about)

11. Knowledgeable (loves to learn and impart their expertise)

12. Leader (leading by example)

Notice to Barbers:

A "TRUE" PROFESSIONAL WHO VALUES "PREPARATION" IS ALWAYS PREPARED...

* to meet any (hair) challenges
* to handle any client demands
* to offer his knowledge and expertise
* to go that extra mile
* to ensure themselves and others receive the best possible service and price
* to make themselves available for their clients
* to be PROFESSIONAL and courteous at all times

P - preparation
R - reinforces
O - opportunities
F - for
E - effective
S - solutions
S - surpassing
I - inferences
O - on
N - networking
A - advancement &
L - learning

A "TRUE" (Hair) Professional is ALWAYS Prepared..

Marcel like any 2-year old was eating after he got dressed,
When his Parents came in to see if he was making a mess.
They noticed his braids had grown nevertheless,
And maybe it was time to trim down the excess.
They approached Marcel to assess his mood,
On cutting his hair and his attitude.

NOTES TO PARENTS:

DO approach and assess the attitude and ability of the barber with cutting Children beforehand. DO NOT choose a barber just because it's near and convenient, search for a PROFESSIONAL.

The Parents discussed Marcel going to get his first haircut,
and how they would decide to bring it up.
They talked and laughed awhile with banter,
although they feared they already knew the answer.
Marcel was fearful of barbers, clippers and razors,
The noises and sounds had caused this behavior.
So the Parents decided to make a stop,
past a barbershop they noticed near the thrift shop.

NOTES TO PARENTS:

DO have banter with barbers in barbershops and be mindful of bad behaviors near or around your children. DO NOT do business with barbers and or barbershops that have questionable clientele and bad behaviors.

The Parents had done many barbershop tours,
and headed home to talk some more.
This time they wanted Marcel to participate,
To see if he would collaborate.
Marcel was adamant about his hair they learned,
and this made his Parents concerned.
For if they couldn't communicate and corroborate,
then how would they ever get the matter straight.

NOTES TO PARENTS:

DO have a conversation and communicate your concerns with the child and barber. DO NOT allow your child to be among barbers and barbershops that are not caring and conducive to your child's overall development.

My Child's First Haircut

A Preparation Tool for
Children, Parents, and Barbers

Dd

Later that day Dad had an idea,
to visit a barbershop to get things clear.
It was just by the bookshop on the harbor,
near the coffeehouse on Arbor.
The Parents thought why not go to the source,
to answer some questions about this discourse.
They had dialogue and good discussion,
On what they could do without a disruption.

NOTES TO PARENTS:

DO have a discourse, discussion and dialogue with the barbers, clients and businesses near and around the barber and barbershop. DO NOT go just because it looks and seems to be ok.

OPEN

Jiz The Barber
JIZTHEBARBER.COM

9

Dad headed to the barbershop with moderate aspirations,
in search of answers and explanations.
He called ahead and introduced himself,
and wanted to speak with JIZ for help.
Dad knew he was talking to a Master Barber with years of
training, for he was attentive, entertaining and engaging.
He talked with knowledge and common sense,
a skilled professional with experience.

NOTES TO PARENTS:

DO decide to choose a Professional with years of experience who is engaged in delivering an experience above your expectations. DO NOT just show up and surprise the Professional he may be busy and unable to give you his full undivided attention.

JIZ is a wise and friendly man who spoke intensely,
and encouraged the Dad to persuade Marcel gently.
JIZ offered him this book so humbly and modest,
to read to him and be open and honest.
The book was forthright, funny and flexible,
And easy to read with answers that were accessible.

NOTES TO PARENTS:

DO be forthright and flexible with your child about what to expect, it should be a fun and friendly experience. DO NOT try to force them into the shop and barber chair, the child will develop a fear complex.

Dad accepted the gift and headed back to the house,
to read and discuss it with his child and spouse.
Marcel was grateful for his new book,
and the act of giving selflessly it took.
As he opened the book to explore what it documented,
the ideas, characters and message were well-presented.
Marcel was engaged since the reading was done,
thinking the book and pictures were colorful and fun.
His Parents started to believe that his haircut might
actually get done.

NOTES TO PARENTS:

DO be genuine and gratuitous by giving your child a goal that they can gain. DO NOT give them a complex by not preparing them for what they are about to experience, this is a FIRST for them.

Marcel was excited he had finished his new book,
it was helpful and hopeful toward his new outlook.
He was open to his first haircut with no contest,
and his Parents were happy the book had
delivered as promised.

NOTES TO PARENTS:

DO be honest and hopeful that your child will be just as excited as you are to get their haircut. DO NOT enlist the services of a barber or barbershop that is not helpful in making this a happy outcome for all.

Marcel grabs his new book as he was inspired,
to get his haircut with the information he had acquired.
His Parents admired his new initiative,
for the book he was given was very informative.
Marcel's Parents had a new tool to help foster his development,
so they made an appointment for the momentous event.

NOTES TO PARENTS:

DO look for a Professional that is informative and inspiring and takes the initiative when dealing with your child. DO NOT intentionally let someone influence you into letting incompetent individuals cut your child's hair and who has no interest in their well-being and the overall impact this could have on their growth-they only see the income$.

Marcel and his Parents took off on their journey,
to see JIZ for their appointment at 5:30.
On the car ride Marcel surveys his new book,
excited about getting his new look.
JIZ reassured the Parents on this joint-venture,
that Marcel would treasure this new adventure.
For Marcel thought if I just sit still,
That all would be fine, fun and joyful.

NOTES TO PARENTS:

DO be joyful on this journey and joint-venture with your child. DO NOT jump on them if they are still a little scared. DO NOT justify improper planning and preparation as just another reason to jump into anyone chair-you might regret it.

They arrived at the barbershop 5:20 that Wednesday,
On a day of the week when it's less of a frenzy.
But just as they came upon the doorway entry,
the Parents encouraged Marcel again real gently.
Marcel looked into the barbershop directly,
he could see books and toys that were kid-friendly.
This gave Marcel and his Parents peace of mind,
of worrying and whether to say nevermind.
The people inside seemed kind and approachable,
just like the book said it wasn't so terrible.

NOTES TO PARENTS:

DO look for an environment and barber that is kid-friendly. DO NOT be to keen on keeping you and your child from knowing and seeing other kids interacting in the barbershop environment-knowledge is power.

My Child's
First Haircut
A Psychological Tool for
Children, Parents, and Barbers

by John E. Bey, Jr

POWDER

IZTHEBARBER.COM

Once inside they didn't feel leary,
they were greeted and seated and it was inviting and cheery.
Marcel and his Parents gave the place a look-over,
and compared it to the book before JIZ came over.
It was exactly the kind of place that you could look up to,
that wasn't just about ego and revenue.
For the Parents this should be a major requirement,
to choose a loving and learning environment.

NOTES TO PARENTS:

DO look for a loving learning environment for your child in the barber and barbershop you choose. DO NOT leave it up to chance, be leery of questionable barbers and environments and look-over the place to ensure it is fun and safe for you and your child.

As soon as the Parents had confirmed all of their answers,
they realized that this must be the standard.
A place where there are no bad attitudes,
a kid-friendly environment that exudes gratitude.
Marcel was so involved in his new book reading,
to even notice that JIZ was speaking.
But as he stood up and minded his manners,
JIZ greeted him again and they shook hands right after.
JIZ is a big guy that has a big black beard,
when Marcel and JIZ connected he made his fears
disappear.

NOTES TO PARENTS:

DO have a meeting with the barber at the barbershop to monitor his mood, manners, and morals; they must model good behaviors. DO NOT make exceptions to this standard.

JIZTHEBARBER.COM

Jiz

POWDER

27

JIZ and Marcel begin to discuss the book,
and how long each haircut had took.
They laughed and talked and bonded early,
because JIZ had shown himself to be trustworthy.
The Parents must insist on this type of framework,
and seek out a Barber who networks around teamwork.
JIZ and Marcel were like long lost friends,
a common bond you should build with all new clients.
Marcel and his Parents were so victorious,
for acquiring knowledge of this new experience.
For the barber and child bond-building must exist,
so that they will never forget it.

NOTES TO PARENTS:

DO be neighborly and network with your barber for this is a new opportunity for him to gain a new client. DO NOT assume the child and barber will automatically vibe, you must negotiate when needed.

Jiz

IIZTHEBARBER.COM

Oo

JIZ showed Marcel around at his requests,
he wanted there to be openness.
It helped Marcel overcome his obstacles and fears,
offering opportunities to build and bond for years.
Marcel learned all about the barber's tools and equipment,
Because JIZ explained it over with consistence.

NOTES TO PARENTS:

DO allow opportunities to overcome obstacles and fears by offering openness and honesty. DO NOT overlook opportunities to build and bond with the barber and child.

Jiz

JIZTHEBARBER.COM

My Child's
First Haircut

Pp

Marcel expressed his thanks so nice and polite,
For the book had provided advice and insight.
It offer ways for Marcel to cope with fears so practical,
With pictures, words and numbers that are understandable.
The Parents were humbled by something so personal,
Like JIZ conducting himself as a professional.
He showed Marcel over to his work station,
and what it means by preparation.

NOTES TO PARENTS:

DO try to prepare and practice politeness with your child toward the barber professional. DO NOT let professionalism go unnoticed.

JIZ explained and answered Marcel's questions,
as he prepared him for the shampoo session.
Marcel braids were long and thick,
his mom helped undo them quick.
Marcel sat real still and quaint,
As JIZ shampooed with no complaint.
A shampoo before cutting is quid pro quo,
when Marcel got done he had a big wet Afro.

NOTES TO PARENTS:

DO shampoo the child's hair thoroughly before coming to the barbershop, or allow the barber to do it. DO NOT put any grease or pomade in the child's hair, this can be done after it has been cut and styled.

JIZ then walked Marcel to the barber chair to relax,
to blow dry his hair and cut it exact.
This also can be done by the Parents before,
you come to the shop most barbers prefer.
Put no oil, lotion, or grease on them,
only after they get it cut or trimmed.
JIZ had made it feel so normal,
and the novel made it so insightful.
The book reinforces good qualities, behavior and morals,
A teaching tool with useful resources.

NOTES TO PARENTS:

DO try and condition your child to the feel and sound of a blow dryer as this may be a challenge in the barber's chair. DO NOT blow dry the hair too straight or use excessive heat as this can cause the hair to stand up and be harder to lay down if they are getting a close cropped hairstyle.

JIZ began cutting Marcel being careful and sensitive,
Because clippers can get hot and barbers heavy-handed.
Parents don't be angry if the child is not submissive,
Encourage them to be still, be more subtle and supportive.
Remember this can be unfamiliar and awkward,
That's why you should be so straight forward.
JIZ continued to work his art,
He wanted Marcel to be stylish and sharp.

NOTES TO PARENTS:

DO be mindful that your child may not sit still during some aspects of the haircut. Therefore, you must be sensitive and supportive with the child and barber to complete the process. DO NOT let the barber shapeup the child if the hair is really fine and thin around the hairline, it is still growing in. If you do, have the barber shape up the fine hair as far out as possible, whereas it might not be clearly visible. FOR ONCE IT'S GONE, IT MAY NOT GROW BACK.

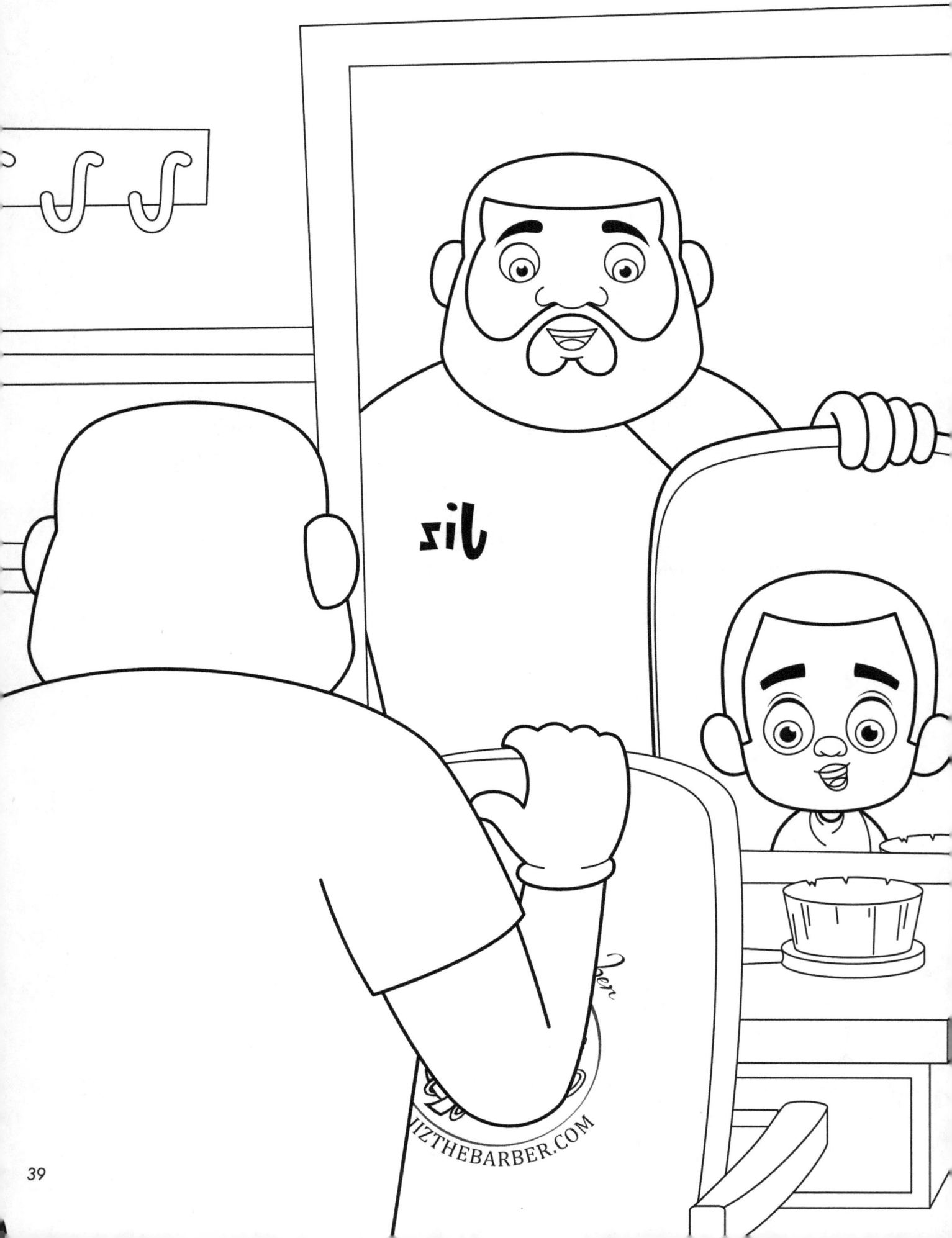

JIZ gave the Parents exactly what they wanted,
A true professional with lots of talent.
They admired the way he didn't rush,
A time sensitive barber that they could trust.
Just like the book had documented,
JIZ THE BARBER had represented.
A Master Barber who's gentle with his tools and razor,
And conscious that the Parents are also team players.
JIZ turned the chair toward the mirror by the handle,
And Marcel smiled and his Parents were thankful.

NOTES TO PARENTS:

DO your homework and look around and wait till you find a Barber Professional, someone who is not only talented but tender, time sensitive and team-oriented. DO NOT let your child's first experience be a reminder to him of how future visits will be. This first experience is about TRUST, he expects that from YOU and the Barber.

Marcel was brave during his first haircut upstanding,
And the barber was patient and understanding.
For there is no other enhancement technique,
Other than to be unique.
Marcel then told JIZ up-top,
High-fiving as he received a lollipop.
JIZ also presented him with a certificate,
For bravery at its ultimate.

NOTES TO PARENTS:

DO make a big deal when it's all over rewarding his new experience, it is of the utmost importance. DO NOT leave without a picture, certificate or lock of hair to remember this unique ultimate undertaking.

My Child's
First Haircut

This is to Certify that

By
Barber's Name

IT'STHEBARBER.COM

43

Marcel's Parents voiced congratulations for taking his haircut so serious,
And that made Marcel feel victorious.
In actuality JIZ and the book were really valuable,
In making his first haircut seem so practical.
For its not about the glitz, glamour or the dollar,
But all about the PREPARATION and VALOR.

NOTES TO PARENTS:

DO voice your admiration and satisfaction to your child and barber for achieving this milestone. DO NOT leave the barbershop without booking your next appointment and tipping, Barbers like waitresses do rely on their tips.

As Marcel and his Parents waved goodbye,
They marveled how JIZ had made it worthwhile.
For Marcel wanted to repeat it somehow,
And his Parents just remarked with "WOW."
Because if not for the book they were given,
This might not have been such a win-win.

NOTES TO PARENTS:

DO support your barber's entrepreneurial endeavors. DO NOT leave without your child shaking hands or saying goodbye to their barber, this will help to solidify their bond until their next appointment.

Marcel was so excited and curious,
To come and see JIZ for another experience.
He marveled at the stations and formulations,
For it was more than his wildest expectations.
His Parents had found JIZ to be such a Professional,
They booked Marcel every (2) weeks on his schedule.
The book JIZ gave them was such a testament,
An excellent tool in this phase of development.

NOTES TO PARENTS:

DO make sure to schedule your child's appointment on a consistent basis, usually every (2) or (3) weeks. DO NOT schedule your child on a barber's busy days if possible, this is to make sure your child will have their undivided attention in case the child is not having a good hair day.

Now back at home the Parents thought it significant,
To capture the moment with pictures for his certificate.
Marcel passed his rite of passage from child to young man,
With a tool and guidance he could understand.
Marcel's Parents were pleased with his new look,
And looked forward to the companion Coloring Book.
They both will help someone to overcome,
The fear of "firsts" for years to come.
So don't you worry not in the least bit,
If Marcel didn't quit,
then that means you too can do it..!

NOTES TO PARENTS:

DO take plenty of pictures and let the barber capture it also for his own collection. DO NOT forget to collect some of the child's hair to place on the certificate if so desired, the certificate should reflect a before and after haircut.

51

The next day at daycare all the other children admired Marcel's new haircut and he was proud that he had conquered his fear and accomplished his goal of getting his "first" haircut.

The moral of the story that JIZ and Marcel want you to know is that.."There is nothing we cannot do with a little Love, Commitment and PREPARATION."

THE END

My Child's First Haircut

JIZTHEBARBER.COM

This is to Certify that

_____

Name

Has Achieved HIS/HER
First Haircut
on

_____

Date

Before

After

By

_____

Barber's Name

My Child's First Haircut

LIZTHEBARBER.COM

This is to Certify that

_____

Name

Has Achieved HIS/HER
First Haircut
on

_____

Date

Before

After

By

_____

Barber's Name

www.ingramcontent.com/pod-product-compliance
Lightning Source LLC
Chambersburg PA
CBHW081341090426
42737CB00017B/3237